VANCOUVER
CANUCKS

BY WILLIAM ARTHUR

Book design by Maggie Villaume
Cover design by Maggie Villaume

Photographs ©: Darryl Dyck/The Canadian Press/AP Images, cover, 8, 23; Jason Franson/The Canadian Press/AP Images, 4–5; Michael Dwyer/AP Images, 7; Matty Zimmerman/AP Images, 10–11; Fred Jewell/AP Images, 13; Graig Abel/Getty Images Sport/Getty Images, 14; Mark J. Terrill/AP Images, 16–17; Michael Tweed/AP Images, 19; Leon Algee/AP Images, 20; Chuck Stoody/The Canadian Press/AP Images, 24–25; Marcio Jose Sanchez/AP Images, 27; Craig Lassig/AP Images, 29

Press Box Books, an imprint of Press Room Editions.

ISBN
978-1-63494-596-7 (library bound)
978-1-63494-614-8 (paperback)
978-1-63494-649-0 (epub)
978-1-63494-632-2 (hosted ebook)

Library of Congress Control Number: 2022913236

Distributed by North Star Editions, Inc.
2297 Waters Drive
Mendota Heights, MN 55120
www.northstareditions.com

Printed in the United States of America
Mankato, MN
012023

ABOUT THE AUTHOR

William Arthur is a sportswriter and author who grew up playing hockey on a frozen pond in Thunder Bay, Ontario. He lives in northwest Ontario with his trusted foxhound, Terry.

TABLE OF CONTENTS

1

Elias Pettersson
(left) hugs Tanner
Pearson after a
Canucks goal in
the 2020 playoffs.

A NEW CORE

Nothing about the 2020 Stanley Cup playoffs was normal. COVID-19 had spread around the world. The National Hockey League (NHL) was forced to suspend its season in March. By the time play resumed in August, the world had changed. For the Vancouver Canucks, however, the season remained one of opportunity.

In the shortened 69-game season, the Canucks won 36 games. That marked the team's first winning season in five years. After the break, games resumed in two cities, but without the fans. The Canucks and 11 other teams went to Edmonton.

Vancouver met the Minnesota Wild in a best-of-five play-in series. The Wild won Game 1. Six points from defenseman Quinn Hughes helped Vancouver win the next three games. The St. Louis Blues were up next. The Blues were the defending Stanley Cup champions. That didn't intimidate the Canucks. The teams went toe to toe. The Canucks won Game 1. Center Bo Horvat scored the overtime winner for the Canucks

Quinn Hughes finished second in the Calder Memorial Trophy voting after the 2019–20 season. The Calder is given to the league's best rookie.

in Game 2. Another win in Game 5 put Vancouver up 3–2. Then the Canucks got off to a hot start in Game 6.

Midway through the second period, the Canucks went on a power play. Center Elias Pettersson received a pass along the sideboards. He sent the puck to Hughes

Brock Boeser dons the "Black Skate" sweater in a 2020 game against the New York Rangers.

at the blue line. Hughes then turned it to winger Brock Boeser atop the far face-off circle. Boeser unleashed a one-timer. The puck screamed past the Blues' goalie for a 4–0 lead. Vancouver went on to win 6–2. But that fourth goal stood out.

That's because the three key players were all 22 or younger. It seemed that the Canucks were building a solid core of young players.

Vancouver pressed on. A competitive series against the Vegas Golden Knights reached Game 7. However, a 3–0 shutout by the Golden Knights finally ended the Canucks' run.

Still, Canucks fans were feeling hopeful. With Boeser, Hughes, and Pettersson, a new generation looked ready to take over.

50 SEASONS

The 2019–20 season marked the Canucks' 50th in the NHL. The team celebrated its history throughout. One way it did that was by wearing retro uniforms. Among them was the famous "Black Skate" sweater from the 1990s.

2

Lester Patrick (center) poses with his sons Murray (left) and Lynn in 1955.

WESTERN HOCKEY

Pro hockey has a long history in Vancouver. In 1911, brothers Lester and Frank Patrick created the Pacific Coast Hockey Association (PCHA). Three teams played in British Columbia. The NHL did not yet exist. The Stanley Cup did, though. And in 1915, the Vancouver Millionaires won the famous trophy. As of 2022, they were still the city's lone championship team.

However, the PCHA disbanded in 1924. The Millionaires folded two years later. For the next several decades, Vancouver had only minor league hockey.

The NHL was founded in 1917. From 1942 to 1967, the league included just six teams. It doubled in size in the 1967–68 season. Two more teams joined in 1970. One was the Buffalo Sabres. The other was the Vancouver Canucks. They became the NHL's first team in western Canada.

Fans came out to support the team early on. But the Canucks didn't do much winning. In 1974–75, they posted their first winning record. The team reached the

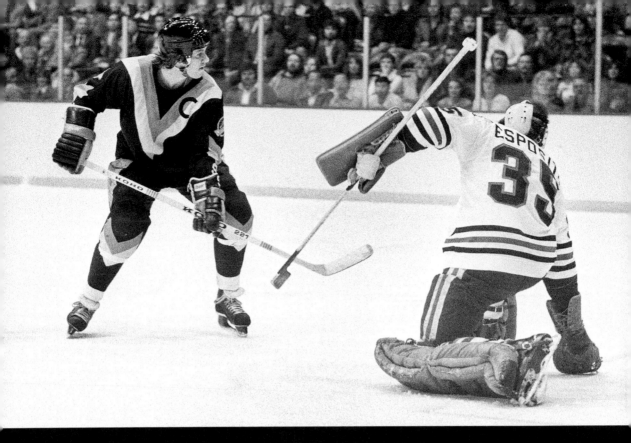

playoffs in 1975 and 1976. However, its losing ways returned soon after.

There was reason for hope, though. In 1978, the Canucks picked Stan Smyl in the draft. At 5-foot-8 and 185 pounds, the right winger didn't stand out much. But he

Stan Smyl's eight-year run as the Canucks' captain was matched only by Henrik Sedin in the 2010s.

had grit and a soft scoring touch. By 1979 the Canucks were a playoff team again. And Smyl was their key player.

In 1981–82, Vancouver ended the season on a nine-game unbeaten streak. The Canucks stayed hot into the playoffs. They won a playoff series for the first time. Then they won two more. Just like that, Smyl and the Canucks were in the Stanley Cup Final. However, a dominant New York Islanders team awaited. They swept the Canucks as part of a four-year run atop the NHL.

WHAT'S A CANUCK?

There was little question as to what Vancouver's NHL team would be named. A minor league team called the Canucks had been around since 1945. But what's a Canuck? The name dates back to a political cartoon started in 1869. One of the characters was named Johnny Canuck. Eventually Canuck became a slang term for Canadian.

3

Pavel Bure
scored 254 goals
in seven seasons
with Vancouver.

BUILDING
UP

The Canucks named Stan Smyl captain before the 1982–83 season. But the team struggled to build on its playoff run. By 1991, the Canucks had played 21 seasons. They had a winning record in just two of them.

A turnaround was in the works, though. Former Canucks player Pat Quinn returned in 1987 as general manager. He quickly traded for goalie Kirk McLean. The team drafted forward Trevor Linden second overall in 1988. It took a chance on Pavel Bure late in the next year's draft. Before long Linden was the team captain. In 1991, Bure arrived from his native Soviet Union. One year later, the speedy winger scored 60 goals.

The Canucks won their division in 1992 and 1993. But they played their best in the 1994 playoffs. Vancouver met the favored Calgary Flames in the first round. The Canucks won Games 5 and 6 in overtime. Then Game 7 went to overtime, too. McLean made 46 saves in the game. At one point, the Flames sprang a three-on-one breakaway. McLean slid skates-first across the goal to snuff it out.

To Canucks fans, the play is known simply as "The Save." Then Bure ended the series with a breakaway goal of his own in the second overtime.

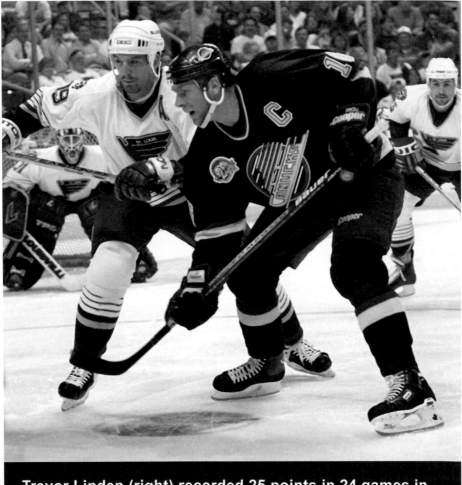

Trevor Linden (right) recorded 25 points in 24 games in the 1994 playoffs.

That ignited the underdog Canucks.

Soon they were in the Stanley Cup Final.

The New York Rangers were favored.

Game 1 was in New York. Behind 52 saves from McLean, Vancouver won in overtime. The Rangers took the next three. But the Canucks rallied to tie the series. That set up Game 7 back in New York. Both teams were desperate to win. Linden scored twice for the Canucks. But it was not enough. The Rangers won 3–2. Once again that proved the high point for this group of Canucks. But better times were coming again soon.

"CAPTAIN CANUCK"

Trevor Linden played 19 NHL seasons. All but three of them included at least some time in Vancouver. A beloved player in the city, Linden served seven years as team captain. After two stints with the team, "Captain Canuck" retired as Vancouver's leader in games played and assists.

THE SEDINS

Going into the 1999 NHL Draft, the Canucks made a series of trades. With the second overall pick, they selected Swedish forward Daniel Sedin. One pick later, they choose his twin brother, Henrik Sedin. The moves to get both brothers paid off in a big way.

Henrik, a center, was best known for his playmaking. His slick passes led to many assists. Daniel, who played left wing, was the scorer. Their chemistry was unmatched.

In 2009–10, Henrik won the Art Ross Trophy. It's given to the NHL player with the most points in a season. One year later, Daniel won it. Henrik also won the Hart Memorial Trophy as the NHL's Most Valuable Player in 2010.

After 17 seasons, the brothers retired together in 2018. One of the two holds almost every Canucks career offensive record.

Henrik (left) and Daniel Sedin
both played all 17 seasons of
their careers in Vancouver.

4

Todd Bertuzzi
celebrates
scoring against
the Detroit
Red Wings in a
2005 game.

BACK TO THE CUP

Things bottomed out for Vancouver in 1998–99. The Canucks won just 23 of 82 games. Trevor Linden had been traded by then. The Canucks moved on from Pavel Bure that January.

The early 2000s brought new life to Vancouver. Wingers Markus Näslund and Todd Bertuzzi arrived in the late 1990s. The team traded for center Brendan Morrison in 2000. Their "West Coast Express" line became one of the NHL's best. But early playoff exits became the norm.

The Canucks needed to build a new core. Daniel and Henrik Sedin proved to be the perfect cornerstones. The twin brothers from Sweden debuted in 2000. By the end of the decade, they were two of the league's most dynamic players. The Canucks built a strong team around them. Center Ryan Kesler could both score and defend. Roberto Luongo was a top goalie.

In 2010–11, Vancouver charged to its first Presidents' Trophy. The trophy is

INTERNATIONAL HOCKEY

The Canucks opened the 1997–98 season in unfamiliar territory. They played the Mighty Ducks of Anaheim in Tokyo, Japan. It was the first time the NHL hosted a regular-season game outside of North America. The Canucks won 3–2.

Roberto Luongo makes a save during the 2011 playoffs.

awarded to the team with the league's
best record. The Canucks then battled
through three playoff series to reach the
Stanley Cup Final. No Canadian team
had won the Cup in 18 years. The Boston

Bruins weren't about to make it easy, though. The series went all the way to Game 7. But on Vancouver's ice, the Bruins dominated 4–0 to win the Cup.

The Canucks won another Presidents' Trophy the next season. However, a first-round playoff exit followed. There was still reason for optimism. Center J. T. Miller emerged as a star. He was eventually joined by young defenseman Quinn Hughes and forwards Elias Pettersson and Brock Boeser. The Canucks returned to the playoffs in 2020.

Rising to the top of the NHL isn't easy, however. After a rough season and a half, the Canucks brought in Bruce Boudreau as coach late in 2021. The team

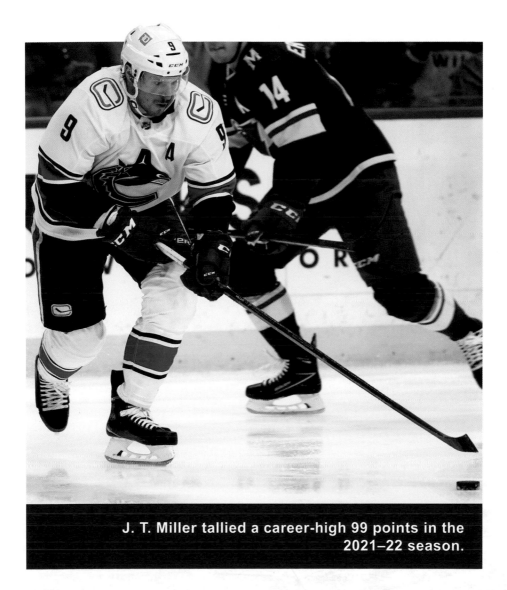

J. T. Miller tallied a career-high 99 points in the 2021–22 season.

improved after the change. Fans hoped this new group could bring the Cup back to Vancouver.

• VANCOUVER CANUCKS
QUICK STATS

FOUNDED: 1970

STANLEY CUP CHAMPIONSHIPS: 0

KEY COACHES:

- Pat Quinn (1991–94, 1996), 141 wins, 111 losses, 28 ties

- Marc Crawford (1999–2006), 246 wins, 189 losses, 62 ties, 32 overtime losses

- Alain Vigneault (2006–13), 313 wins, 170 losses, 57 overtime losses

HOME ARENA: Rogers Arena (Vancouver, BC)

MOST CAREER POINTS: Henrik Sedin (1,070)

MOST CAREER GOALS: Daniel Sedin (393)

MOST CAREER ASSISTS: Henrik Sedin (830)

MOST CAREER SHUTOUTS: Roberto Luongo (38)

Stats are accurate through the 2021–22 season.

GLOSSARY

CAPTAIN
A team's leader.

DEBUT
First appearance.

DYNAMIC
Energetic, creating positive change.

GENERAL MANAGER
The person in charge of a sports team, whose duties include signing and trading players.

ONE-TIMER
A shot taken by a player who both receives a pass and shoots the puck all in one motion.

POWER PLAY
A situation in which one team has more players on the ice because an opposing player is serving a penalty.

RETRO
A style that calls back to the past.

• TO LEARN MORE

BOOKS

Davidson, B. Keith. *NHL*. New York: Crabtree Publishing, 2022.

Duling, Kaitlyn. *Women in Hockey*. Lake Elmo, MN: Focus Readers, 2020.

Graves, Will. *Ultimate NHL Road Trip*. Minneapolis: Abdo Publishing, 2019.

MORE INFORMATION

To learn more about the Vancouver Canucks, go to **pressboxbooks.com/AllAccess**.

These links are routinely monitored and updated to provide the most current information available.

INDEX